Dedicated
to the Father of mercies.
Whose grace is
wonderfully unfair.

KIDDERMINSTER KINGDOM TALES
King Leonard's Celebration
Sir Humphrey's Honeystands
Nicholas and His Neighbors
Cornelius T. Mouse and Sons
King Leonard's Great Grape Harvest
Mrs. Beaver and the Wolf at the Door

1 2 3 4 5 6 7 8 9 10 Printing/Year 94 93 92 91

ISBN: 0-89693-268-0

VICTOR BOOKS
A division of SP Publications, Inc.
Wheaton, Illinois 60187

King Leonard's Great Grape Harvest

In the Kingdom of Kidderminster there was a lion king who ruled over all the beasts. His name was Leonard, and he lived in a majestic castle high atop a mountain in the center of a jungle.

Leonard was a very good king and greatly enjoyed doing gracious things for his subjects. It pleased him to give the animals of his kingdom food to eat and clothes to wear. On some occasions he would send his servants down into the jungle to deliver barrels of coconuts and to leave brightly colored jackets and scarves at the animals' homes. When the jungle residents were in need of shoes for their little ones, King Leonard would summon his royal shoemakers and have them craft tiny sneakers, sandals, and loafers. At his command the shoemakers would deposit them on the doorsteps of the jungle residents. The king would watch through his royal telescope as youngsters bounced about with joy in their new shoes.

One bright afternoon in the fall of the year, as King Leonard sat on his throne looking out across the jungle through his royal telescope, he spied his vineyard. He could see that the twisting grapevines had grown long and tall and were now covered with plump, juicy, purple grapes.

"Horatio!" the king roared.

In a matter of moments a tall, thin bird clothed in a colorful kingdom uniform scurried up to the throne.

"Yes, Sire?" the bird asked with a salute. "How may I be of service to you?"

"I have just noticed that my royal vineyard is full of plump, juicy grapes," King Leonard said, turning his gaze toward the polite servant.

"Congratulations, Sire," the bird smiled warmly. "All the time and effort spent planting and tending the vineyard has yielded you an abundant crop."

"Yes, Horatio," the lion said thoughtfully. "But now, these are special grapes that must be picked in short order, or they shall dry up on the vine."

"Then you would have the greatest supply of raisins in all the land," the bird chuckled.

The king was not amused. His furry face was solemn and his regal nose twitched as he thought about the vineyard.

"I will have your servants attend to it immediately, Sire." The bird bowed. "Your vineyard shall be harvested in a week's time."

"The grapes must be picked tomorrow," the king ordered, "or they will spoil. And if they spoil, I will not be able to give them to my subjects, and my guests will not be able to enjoy them at our celebrations."

"But Sire," the thin bird objected, "not even the host of servants under your charge could do the job. Not even if all your guests helped could it be done. It would take an army of animals."

"Then see to it that an army is assembled, Horatio," the king demanded. "Those grapes must be picked!"

"I will try my best, Sire," the bird sighed, turning to leave.

"One moment," the king said, holding out his large paw. "If this is to be done correctly, perhaps I had best attend to it myself. Prepare my chariot."

"But Sire!" Horatio shouted with wide eyes. "You don't intend to—"

"I certainly do," the king said with a smile. "Tomorrow before the sun rises, I am going down into the jungle, to the marketplace, to hire animals to pick the grapes in my vineyard."

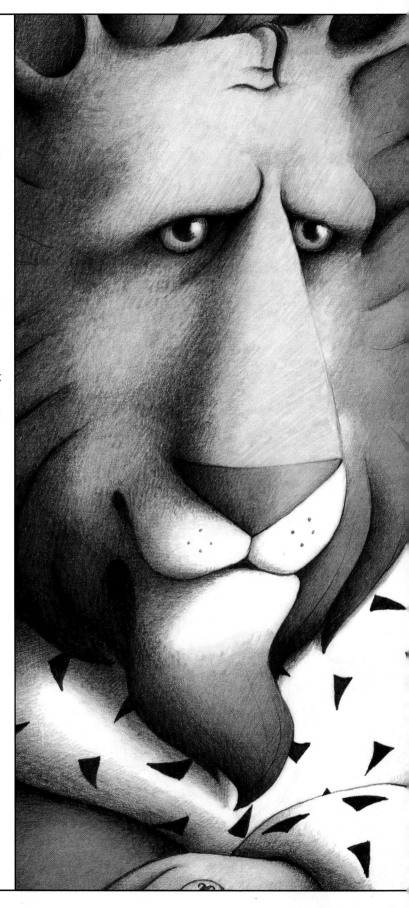

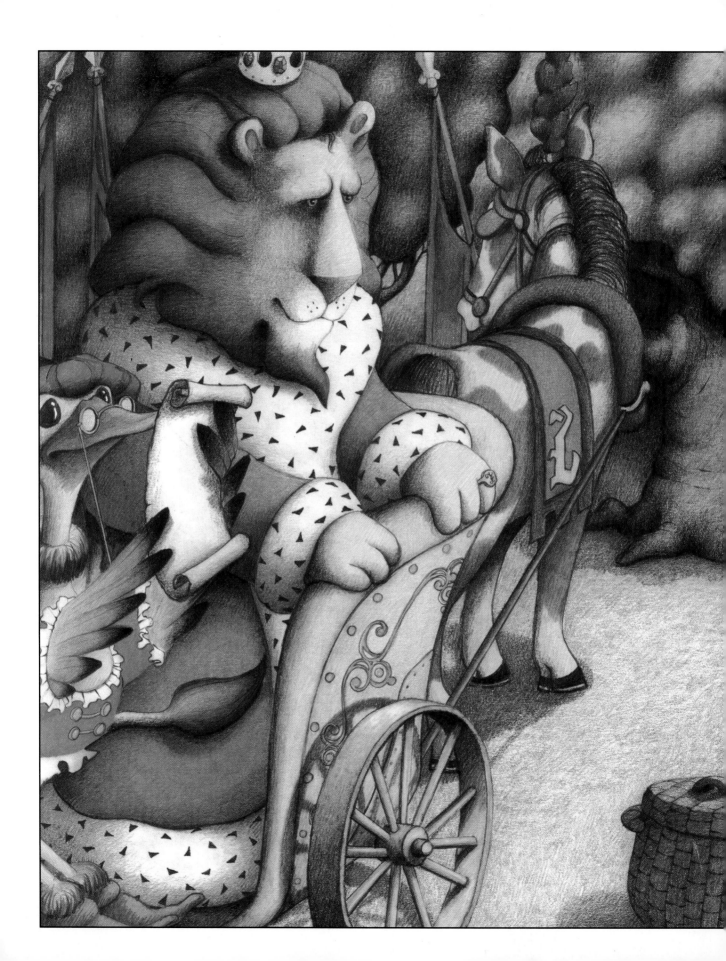

So the royal chariot was prepared, and the next morning at dawn, King Leonard, clothed in a regal robe of shimmering purple, rode down from his majestic castle with Horatio, his loyal servant, by his side. Before them marched a troop of brightly clad trumpeters and animals carrying royal banners. It was barely light when the procession reached the jungle marketplace, but it was already clamoring with activity. A flock of parrots, toucans, and other exotic birds were setting up fruit stands; a pair of snakes were hissing about their leather goods; an orangutan was bouncing up and down on a pile of baskets and pots trying to interest customers in his wares; and a wildebeest was pulling a cartload of baked goods through the square. Animals were everywhere, shopping, talking, and settling in for a day of milling about.

"Stop the chariot!" King Leonard ordered.

The procession came to an abrupt halt and the trumpeters blew out a brilliant note. The marketplace was suddenly still and quiet. All eyes were drawn to the king's chariot.

Horatio rose and lifted his long, thin head to announce the king's arrival. "Hear ye, hear ye, all animals of the jungle," he shouted in a voice much louder than his normal voice. "The good King Leonard has come down from his castle."

A rumble was heard throughout the crowd of animals. Some wondered if this was a joke of some sort; others thought it might be a trick. There were those who were so frightened by the procession that they made straight for their homes. Still others were curious and struggled to get a better look at this king.

Rising from the chariot, King Leonard prepared to speak. The crowd gasped at his size and royal attire, and trembled as he gave a low growl to clear his throat.

"I have come among you today," the king said in a deep, noble voice, "to offer work to those who are willing."

The animals remained silent, their eyes glued on the regal lion.

"To each of those who will go out into my vineyard and pick grapes today," he said, eyeing the crowd, "I will give one silver coin." He held up a shiny coin for the animals to see.

"We already have a job," the snakes hissed. "And business is good."

"Yes, quite good," the orangutan chimed in.

"We don't need your coins," the birds squawked. "We'll stick to our fruit."

"And me to my bread," the wildebeest snorted.

"Why, you impolite, discourteous beasts—" Horatio fumed.

"Now, now." The king held out his paw to the angry bird. "Very well, those of you with work to do, be about it and may you prosper. But what of the rest of you?"

No one spoke.

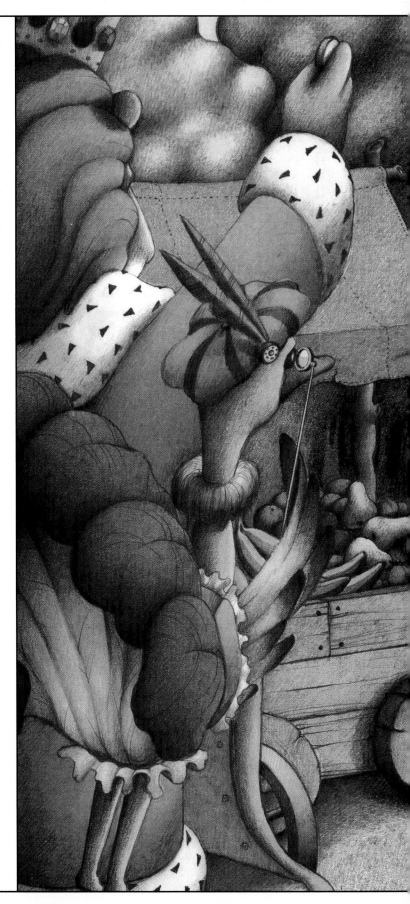

"You there," the king pointed. "My good rhinoceros. Are you occupied today?"

"No, I guess not," the rhinoceros frowned.

"Then work in my vineyard for a silver coin," the king said.

"Why not?" the rhinoceros snorted. "I was just gonna hang around here all day anyway. Might as well make some money."

"Very good," the king said brightly. "Are there others? Are there other animals who would like to take home a silver coin this evening?"

A gorilla grunted his consent, a leopard leapt forward, and a wild boar squealed his approval as a line began to form next to the king's chariot.

"I wonder if they shall be enough to do the job," the king thought aloud after the animals had been led off toward the vineyard by a servant.

"It's hard to say, Sire," Horatio said. "Your vineyard is quite large and there are so many grapes to be picked. Perhaps you should enlist other workers later in the day to be sure that the job will be done before evening."

"A fine idea," the king said, obviously pleased. "I will return every so often and deliver my offer for those who might have missed it. Horatio, have the driver take us once around the jungle."

After the tall, thin bird had relayed the king's request, the procession began to march forward.

It took King Leonard's chariot the better part of three hours to travel all the way around the jungle, and when they arrived back at the marketplace the king was pleased to find a whole new group of animals. Among the traders, farmers, and barterers was a collection of animals who stood about looking bored.

"Halt!" the king commanded and the royal trumpeters gave a long toot on their horns.

"Why are you animals standing about doing nothing?" King Leonard asked.

"Nothin' to do," a giraffe answered. "We don't have jobs."

"You do now, if you wish," he said. "Come, work in my vineyard and receive a silver coin."

The animals raised their eyebrows as they looked at the shiny coin in the lion's paw and then fell into line behind his chariot and were led away by another servant.

"Another batch of workers to help pick my grapes," King Leonard grinned. "We'll have those grapes picked in no time."

Horatio was about to agree with the king when a royal messenger approached and spoke a word in his ear.

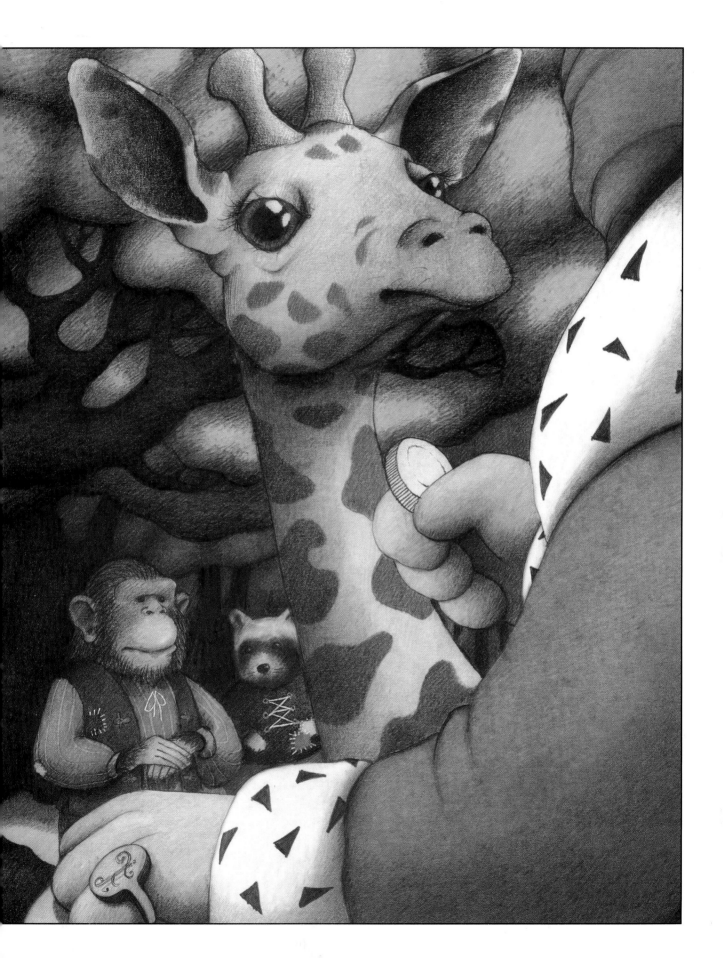

"I have received news from the vineyard, Sire," the thin bird said, turning to face his king.

"Very well," the king said, rubbing his paws together excitedly, "speak it."

"Your servants and the workers you have hired are doing an excellent job picking the grapes," the thin bird began.

"I knew they would," the king beamed. "By tomorrow we'll have enough grapes to fill the entire jungle. My subjects will have all of the plump, juicy fruit they can eat."

"But . . . " Horatio frowned, "there are still many, many vines to harvest. They will not be able to finish the job today, Sire."

King Leonard let out a long sigh and wrinkled up his nose, obviously disappointed.

"Those grapes will spoil by tomorrow," he said. "We must find more workers. Take us around the jungle once again."

"As you wish, Sire." Horatio bowed.

So the royal procession traveled around the jungle again. When they arrived back at the marketplace they found still more animals willing to work in the vineyard. This continued all day long. Finally, when it was almost quitting time, he hired one last group of animals and told them to hurry into the vineyard and pick as many grapes as they could before dark.

"Will we succeed, Horatio?" King Leonard asked as he watched the final collection of workers scurry off down the road.

"It will be very close, Sire," the thin bird said, shaking his head. "Whether or not the last grape will be picked before night falls, I cannot say."

Then the waiting began. As the traders and sellers of goods packed up their stands, loaded their carts, and returned home for the night, King Leonard, Horatio, and the royal procession waited in the marketplace. When the square was quiet and empty, and the sun had fallen beneath the horizon, they were still waiting for the workers to return from the vineyard.

Finally a royal messenger rushed up to Horatio and spoke a word into his ear. He said it with such force that the thin bird almost lost his footing and fell from the chariot.

"Sire!" Horatio shouted after regaining his balance. "The grapes, the grapes!"

"Yes, yes," the royal lion asked, "what about them?"

"They've been picked!" he said, flapping his wings. "Every last grape was picked before the sun went down!"

"Hooray!" the king roared, leaping into the air, nearly losing his crown.

"And the workers are returning, Sire," Horatio said, noticing the animals filing into the marketplace.

"So they are," the king said happily.

When they had all gathered around the royal chariot, King Leonard addressed the bunch.

"My good animals," he began, "I am quite pleased to learn that every grape has been picked from my vineyard. You are to be commended for your faithful, diligent work." He then ordered Horatio to pay them, starting with those who were hired last and ending with those who were hired first.

Things progressed smoothly. The animals hired near quitting time and in the late afternoon were quite happy to receive a silver coin for their few hours of grape picking.

But when those hired early in the morning reached the front of the line, they began to frown. Having worked much longer than those hired in the afternoon, they expected to be paid more than just one coin. And when the animals King Leonard had hired first came to claim their money, they actually scowled and muttered their disapproval.

"Those lazy animals who only worked a few hours got paid as much as we did," the rhinoceros snorted, stamping his feet and raising his horn into the air.

"Yeah, and they didn't pick as many grapes," the leopard whined, his tail standing out straight.

"We should have gotten more than just one coin," the wild boar complained.

"It's not fair!" the gorilla grunted, beating on his chest.

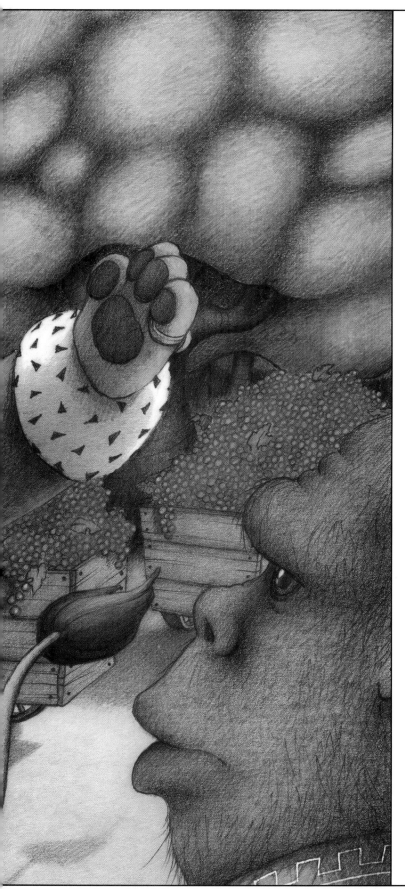

"Not fair, indeed!" King Leonard roared, silencing the grumbling animals. "Did you agree this morning to work in my vineyard for one silver coin?"

"Yes," they nodded.

"Then take your coins and go home," the king said. "I have not cheated you. I have stayed true to my part of the bargain."

"But you can't pay the latecomers as much as you paid us," the rhinoceros objected.

"I am the king," the regal lion growled, glaring at the rhino. "And these are my coins. I can do with them as I wish. Are you upset because I am a kind, generous lion? If I choose to give these animals more than they deserve, what is that to you?"

The grumbling animals didn't say anything this time. They just turned away with pouty expressions on their faces and slowly made for home.

When the square was finally empty, King Leonard had Horatio fetch a clump of grapes. For some time, the regal lion and the tall, thin bird sat in the royal chariot, munching on the sweet fruit and looking at the line of carts stretched across the marketplace, each heaped up high and overflowing with plump, juicy, purple grapes.

"These are quite tasty," the king said.

"Yes, Sire," Horatio agreed. "Crisp and sweet. And we certainly have plenty of them. What will you ever do with so many grapes, Sire?"

"Why, serve some at the palace and give the rest to my subjects, of course," the lion replied.

"But how can you possibly deliver them to all of your subjects?" the thin bird asked.

"Perhaps," the lion said with a gleam in his eye, "perhaps instead of taking the grapes to them, we should bring them to the grapes."

"Sire?" Horatio was puzzled.

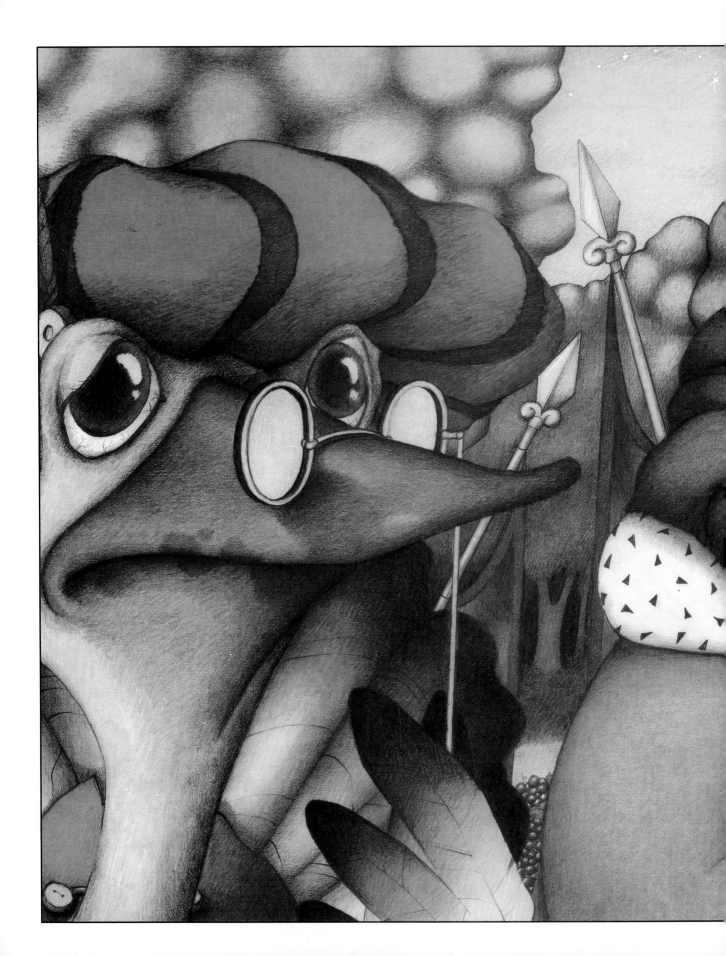

"We'll have a party," the king said excitedly. "Yes, a great grape party for the whole jungle."

"But, Sire—" the bird objected.

"We can have grapes, grape juice, grape jelly . . . " the king continued. "And fine pastries and music . . . Oh . . . and grape ice cream!"

The tall, thin bird covered his eyes with one wing. "Here we go again," he sighed.

"To the castle!" the lion roared. "And be quick about it. These grapes must be washed. There are preparations to make, decorations to be hung, and invitations to be sent out. Oh, there is so much to do! Isn't it exciting, Horatio?"

"Yes, Sire," the bird groaned, "exciting."

And the royal procession began to march in double-time back up to King Leonard's castle in order to make ready a great grape party for the whole jungle.

The End